Henri de Toulouse-Lautrec: self-portrait - 1880 detail - Oil on board, 40.5 x 32.5cm - Albi, Musée Toulouse-Lautrec

TOULOUSE-LAUTREC

"Lautrec's name stands for more than a body of work. It stands for a keenness of mind and sensibility.... for a state of soul which penetrated the hearts of his contemporaries....Like all great visionaries, Lautrec was a precursor. He remains fundamental, like Baudelaire."

E. Schaub-Koch

Toulouse-Lautrec's appearance has become almost as famous as his paintings. He immortalised himself - a tiny, usually immaculately dressed figure hobbling through the bars and brothels of fin-de-siècle Paris - in his many self-caricatures. Lautrec was not in reality **that** tiny - about five feet - but attached to his crippled legs, a mere two feet long, were a normal sized body and a huge head. It seems that he suffered from a rare bone disorder; after breaking both legs in his teens, he ceased to grow any taller and was left with a stunted appearance. Apart from his size, contemporaries commented on his ugliness: "Picture the big head of Gnafron (a grotesque puppet) on the body of a dwarf...greasy oily skin; a nose which would be enough for two faces and a mouth resembling a wound". The pitiless words of Yvette Guilbert, but then there was little pity in some of the many drawings and paintings he did of her. She was to be one of his favourite subjects.

Yet Lautrec never allowed himself to appear discouraged by his physical handicaps; indeed, he often joked about them. He deliberately sought out the company of unusually tall men such as his cousin Gabriel Tapié de Céleyran. He also enjoyed being photographed on bathing trips, even when nude. That he could joke about his appearance so easily is a tribute to his remarkable personality. He charmed all who met him - be it in a chateau or a rough bar - with his energy, his wit and his irrepressible enthusiasms.

Henri Marie Raymond de Toulouse-Lautrec was born in 1864 in Albi in southern France, into a family of ancient nobility who claimed descent from many of the greatest figures in French history, including theoretically Charlemagne and many of the most notable crusaders. Part of Lautrec's effortless assurance is attributable to this background - as also was the wealth which enabled him to enjoy life to the full, without the need to earn a living like most other artists. His father was a notable eccentric, who loved dressing up in bizarre

Aux Ambassadeurs - chromotype, 26 x 22.5cm - "Le Figaro Illustré" July 1893
A typical example of one the many drawings Lautrec did for magazines and newspapers

Photograph of Lautrec, titled "Small Man, Great Artist". Paris, National Library

costumes almost as much as more conventional pleasures such as riding and hunting. He once turned up for a lunch wearing a highland plaid and ballerina's tutu.

Lautrec's mother was a gentle, pious lady who remained devoted to her son, in contrast to his often hostile father. When Lautrec moved to Paris to study under the traditional painter Léon Bonnat in 1882, he lived with his mother for the first four years. His family had supported his precocious talent - Lautrec himself had been taught at home by an artist friend of his father. From Bonnat and from Cormon, to whose studio he moved in 1884, Lautrec learnt the traditional draughtsmanship which was to be the foundation of his style. French painting had experienced an age of immense changes, in which many conventional values had been rejected by the avant garde of the older generation, the Impressionists. It was under the influence of the Impressionists that Lautrec began painting, but he never ignored what he had learnt of traditional skills.

The informal atmosphere of Cormon's classes attracted

many of the most talented young artists in Paris. Here Toulouse met Emile Bernard, a painter of great influence at the end of the decade, and Van Gogh. Lautrec liked the awkward, intense Dutchman and encouraged him to go to Southern France, where he would produce his greatest works. The portrait Lautrec did of Van Gogh, seated alert and observant at a cafe table, remains one of the most vivid images of the artist. Although Lautrec was open to a wide range of influences at this formative stage, the strongest came from Degas, one of the leading Impressionists and 30 years his senior. Degas' elegant, vivid and totally unsentimental views of contemporary life were the starting point for Lautrec's art.

One thing which sharply distinguishes many of Lautrec's works from those of Degas and other earlier painters, is that they were done for posters or lithographs. This helps to explain his distinctively flat colours and calligraphic use of strong outlines, derived in part from his great near-contemporary Paul Gauguin. Undoubtedly more directly influential on the young Lautrec were Japanese prints, which were having such an impact in artistic circles at the time. Strong simple colours and outlines were ideal for the hundreds of posters he would soon be producing.

But the greatest inspiration for Lautrec was perhaps the excitement of the city and especially its night life. After moving into his own studio in Montmartre, he became totally immersed in the low life of the dance halls, cabarets and bars of the neighbourhood. This was a golden age for popular culture with the singers, dancers and comedians who played the cheap venues becoming stars within their own world. Performers like Aristide Bruant, with his broad-brimmed hat and scarf, Yvette Guilbert in a simple green dress and black gloves (see pages 14 and 15) or the skeletally thin dancer Valentin Le Désossé, had larger than life personalities which Lautrec immortalised.

Lautrec made his name celebrating Montmartre life, but he ranged right across the pleasures

Lautrec in his studio while painting Dance At The Moulin Rouge

of the city. As well as the seedy dance halls and brothels - in one of which he took up residence for a while, to study its inhabitants (*The Salon at the Rue Des Moulins,* pages 16,17) - he also visited the classical French theatre, another source of inspiration. He contributed to the high-brow magazine *Revue Blanche*. He was equally passionate about sport, partly due to his father's love of horses and racing. He enjoyed cycling as well, then much in vogue. Although not a great traveller, he visited London in 1895 and later the Low Countries, where his work was exhibited by the group "les XX".

Sadly, over-indulgence in his pleasures began to take their toll. It is almost certain that he had contracted syphilis from one of his encounters; he had also become an alcoholic. As a child he had devoloped a covert taste for alcohol; as an adult he indulged it fully.

In 1899 he spent three months in an asylum after a severe attack of DTs. During his time there he produced some of his most haunting images of circus performers. Despite a temporary recovery, his health was broken by a return

to his bad old ways and he had another collapse two years later. This time there was no recovery and he died in his mother's arms at her country house at Malromé, on 9th of September 1901, at the age of only 37.

Chocolat Dancing At Achille's Bar, *1896 - drawing, 65 x 50cm - Albi, Musée Toulouse-Lautrec*

La Goulue And Valentin Le Désossé, *1894 - lithograph, 29 x 23cm*

BAREBACK RIDER AT FERNANDO'S

1888 - Oil on canvas - 98 x 161 cm,
Chicago, Art Institute

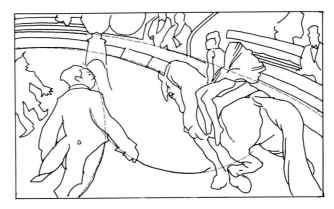

The diagram shows the curved lines that create a sense of circular movement and which instinctively guide Lautrec's composition.

Why did the circus, with its crowded seats and dark interior cut by shafts of light, with its ring for the clowns and acrobats, fascinate so many artists from Seurat and Toulouse-Lautrec to Picasso? What was it that attracted them and made them such admiring spectators? Perhaps it was the dusty atmosphere of a show in which performers risked their lives, perhaps it was the gleam of lights and colours, the movement and the music, or even the subtle melancholy revealed in the performers as soon as the lights went out in the Big Top. Perhaps too the circus symbolised life's spectacle, with its risks and balancings, its laughter and tears, its acrobatics and dreams and, above all, the continual challenge of overcoming every obstacle and every difficulty. This picture, painted by Lautrec in 1888, was the first of a series of paintings inspired by the circus, revealing fully his originality and brilliance.
It is not surprising that when, in 1899, after a violent crisis brought on by drink and reckless living,

Lautrec was forced into a clinic, he rediscovered his love of life through painting from memory a series of works inspired by the circus, his early love. Such vibrant scenes perhaps provided the excitement for a half-crippled Lautrec that sport or warfare had given his crusading ancestors.

TOULOUSE-LAUTREC AND SEURAT
Georges Seurat : The Circus 1890 - 91 - Oil on canvas, 185.5 x 152.5 cm - Paris, Musée d'Orsay.

The same theme - of the circus and an acrobat ballerina - was interpreted in a very different manner by Seurat. The Lautrec is instinctive, immediate and shows no concern for theory; the Seurat is rational, constructed theoretically. Both compositions are based on creating the effect of movement by a series of curved lines (those of the curtain held by the clown in the foreground are typical) which follow one another as in a catherine wheel. But Seurat achieves a very different, much calmer, overall effect with his studied harmony of the yellow-ochre-red tones, rendered through 'divisionism' - the juxtaposition of small brush points of pure colours.

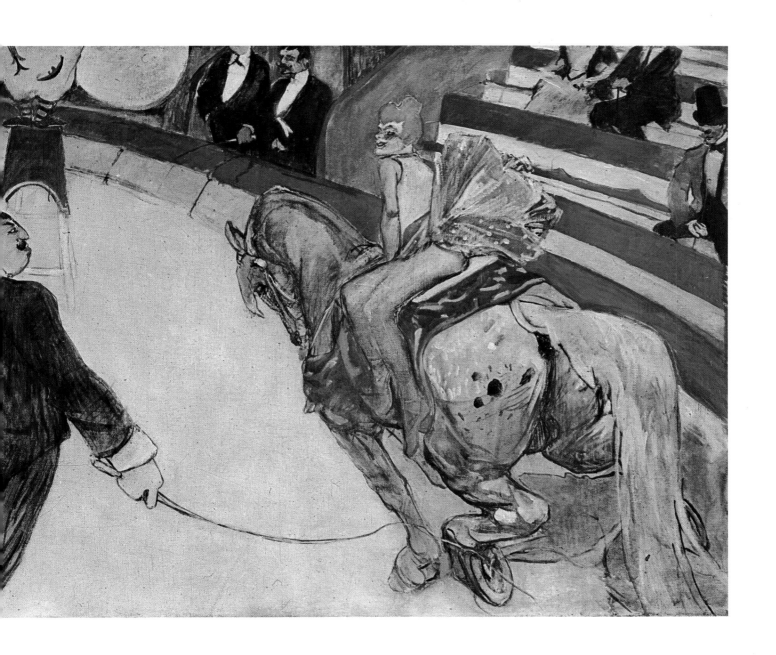

JANE AVRIL DANCING

1892 - Oil on board, 85.5 x 45 cm - Paris, Musée d'Orsay

Toulouse-Lautrec was a careful and faithful witness of the brief but glittering era called the Belle Epoque. He could capture in a fleeting moment the secret thoughts of the characters he recorded. All his work expresses a joie de vivre, despite his deformity and illness, that animates and transforms his drawings, paintings and posters. In his images of the theatre, circus, cabarets and brothels - all haunts of his - Toulouse-Lautrec sings a hymn to life, almost as a victory over the injustice of fate. In the sparkling yet so often selfish and cold world of the music halls, Lautrec's one sincere friend among the female stars was Jane Avril. He was attracted to her graceful and melancholy figure, her sensitive face, her refined elegance at odds with her surroundings. The portrait is painted on board using Lautrec's preferred technique in which the principal figures are depicted in areas of flat colour with the brush strokes thinning out around them until the neutral shade of the board is left as the background tone. This painting illustrates clearly the painter's way of composing and cutting the frame of the picture. The figure is not placed at the centre but, moved towards the left-hand side, seems about to dance off the stage; it is as if she has been caught in mid-movement, moving her legs as she lifts her skirt, preoccupied by the difficulties of the complicated dance of the 'Melinite'.

Against the neutral colour of the board the white of her clothing is contrasted to the blue of her hat, petticoats and stockings, but above all, we are struck by Jane's sad face with its pale melancholy.

Jane Avril Leaves The Moulin Rouge 1892 - Oil on board, 63 x 42 cm Hartford, Wadsworth Atheneum. In contrast to the figures, the background and the street is in almost "pointillist" style.

Jane Avril 1892 - Board, 68 x 53 cm - Washington, National Gallery. Just a few strokes suggest the hat and coat: attention is focused, as always, on the melancholy in the pale face.

AT THE MOULIN ROUGE

1892 - Oil on canvas, 123 x 140 cm - Chicago, Art Institute, Birch Bartlett Collection

At the time of this painting, Impressionism was becoming outdated, and everyone was talking about symbolism or defending the 'cloisonnism' of Bernard and Gauguin (painting that seemed like enamelling), or Seurat's divisionism (he divided a colour into its component shades, placing one next to another in small brush points of different tones). In this atmosphere Toulouse-Lautrec worked alone and independently, without theoretical concerns, devoted above all to the genius of Degas. Lautrec looked to Degas for hints and inspiration. Swept along with the general enthusiasm for the discovery of Japanese art he also studied the refined compositions of Utamaro, Hokusai, Hiroshige and the other masters, allowing himself to be spellbound by their graceful curving lines, the graphic elegance of their design, the basic simplicity of their settings, their innovative composition and the perspective obtained by superimposing planes. The painting *At The Moulin Rouge* is part of the Paris of those years. The Moulin Rouge opened on October 5th 1889 at no.90, Boulevard de Clichy, replacing the dance hall of the 'Reine Blanche'. It advertised itself with a wooden windmill erected over the entrance and inside had a large central dance floor, a 'promenoir' with tables around it, a raised gallery and a garden (later it was to have a small picture gallery as well).
Lautrec paints a section of the 'promenoir' in a foreshortened view - as if the depth of the image is compressed - and in a very cinematographic framing. The influence of the 'composition' of the Japanese prints is also evident. In the foreground is the decisive diagonal of a

The diagram highlights the composition of the painting on the following page (overleaf). The foreground of the balustrade cutting the frame and the figure on the right, strongly illuminated, form the 'wings' - techniques characteristic of a modern film-making style. 'Centre stage' are the characters seated around the table, while in the background the 'extras' mill about.

LA GOULUE
In the background of the painting, seen from behind, is La Goulue, the dancer at the Moulin Rouge who was painted several times by Lautrec (right : At The Moulin Rouge : La Goulue, 1891 - Drawing for a poster - Albi, Musée Toulouse-Lautrec). Very blonde, described by Yvette Guilbert as 'pretty and attractive, but vulgar', La Goulue was a fleeting star of the Paris night. Growing precociously fat, she later became a fairground exhibit.

The Technique

1) Lautrec began the work by sketching the composition of the scene in thick charcoal lines: the balustrade in the foreground, which cuts across the frame diagonally; the figure of the dancer on the right; in the middle, the table with the five figures; in the background other characters, amongst whom is the painter himself.

2) He begins to paint the colours with rapid brushstrokes onto the canvas which is prepared in such a way as to make use of the background tone: first the warm colours - the orange-ochre of

the balustrade, the violet-brown of the coat worn by the man on the left, the ochre of the red-haired lady's dress, the orange of her thick hair.

3) The artist proceeds to cold tones, painting the brown-black of the top hats and the men's clothes and the black-green of the women in the foreground - whose face, illuminated from below, is lit up, framed by her yellow-gold hair, by the transparent blues of the reflected light.

4) He finishes the canvas by painting the other characters and the background wall, using green brushstrokes which let through the canvas tone.

balustrade which draws us into the setting around the principal figures: on the extreme right, like a fantastic mask above dark clothes, is the illuminated yellow and blue of the face of Nelly C.; at the small crowded table, from the left, is the critic Edouard Dujardin, the Spanish dancer Macarona, the photographer Paul Sescan, and the 'bon-viveur' Maurice Guibert with an un-identified lady; in the background La Goulue adjusts her hair in front of the mirror, while Gabriel Tapié de Céleyran walks across with his cousin Toulouse-Lautrec in a bowler hat. The picture documents the life of the time; it is painted with the usual naturalness and immediacy that leads us by the hand 'into' the painter's world.

The face of Nelly C., on the extreme right of the painting (seen on the following page), in a mask transfigured by the light, captured by Lautrec through contrasting the yellow of her hair and of the illuminated areas, and the blue of the reflected areas lit up by the brilliant red of her lips. The whole emerges from the billow of her collar and her black dress.

The framing and style of this poster are of an originality still striking today. An incidental subject - the enormous fingerboard of the double bass - is used as a decorative arabesque that surrounds the whole image. The form of the composition, the stylisation of the musician's hair and distortion of his ear, all are evidence of the interest shown by Lautrec for Art Nouveau, which he helped popularise. The sideview of the stage, accentuated by the lines of the boards, sustains the rhythm of the movement in which the dancer is captured, wrapped in the swirl of her flying skirts. The influence of Japanese prints (much in vogue in Paris at that time) is evident in the use of flat tints and in the drawing of silhouettes without any volume. Essentially three colours are used: red, yellow and grey, heightened by black (the stockings and gloves) and white (the petticoat). Toulouse-Lautrec's interest in the new print-making as a creator of lithograph posters is documented in letters to his mother in 1891:

"Dear Mamma, I am still waiting for my poster to come out - it is suffering from delays in printing but it is very amusing to do. For the first time I have the sensation of being able to exercise authority over an entire workshop...."

And in another dated October of the same year:

"...my poster is today stuck all over the walls of Paris and I am about to make another....".

Preparatory drawing for the poster Jane Avril At The Jardin De Paris, c.1893 - Board, 98 x 70 cm, Paris, private collection.
In Lautrec's work, especially in the lithographs, accessories frequently feature strongly: witness the black stockings worn by Jane.

In the poster for Aristide Bruant his great black hat and red scarf stand out. In Divan Japonais the two figures in the foreground are two pure silhouettes without substance - surfaces of black against which the lively touches of yellow stand out (the stage and the dress of the actress who is Yvette Guilbert; the chair and Jane Avril's bag; the beard and hair of the gentleman).

YVETTE GUILBERT TAKING A CURTAIN CALL

1894 - Lithograph reworked in colour and turpenti
48 x 25 cm - Albi, Musée Toulouse-Lautrec

Among the various series of pictures of theatrical scenes, this image of Yvette taking a bow stands out for its bold framing that draws us in directly as participants. It is also striking for the psychological penetration of the portrait. Toulouse-Lautrec met the actress in 1894 and was impressed by her exceptional talent, her ironic expression and her skill as a cultured and open-minded diseuse (theatrical reciter). Her gangling figure, angular face, pockmarked features, downward-sloping eyebrows, the mouth that seemed like a wound - all attracted him: and Toulouse-Lautrec painted her many times in an attempt to grasp the enigmas of her unsettling personality. Here she is shown bowing to the audience who applaud at the end of a show. Everything here is absolutely new and original: her stance, with her right arm resting on the curtain and the left arm by her side, her body wrapped in the dress, leaning forward slightly, her face raised towards the audience; the light that illuminates her from below; the elongated format, the completely photographic style of framing then totally new.
The principal colour is the watergreen of her dress and of the curtain; against this stands out her figure, lightly drawn, the orangered of the hair, the red of the lips and the pink of the cheeks; above all, the ironic disturbing expression shining out of her made-up eyes. We seem to smell the dust of the stage, hear the applause and feel an urge to join in. Rarely, even when we have seen a show in person, can have we felt so much 'part' of the stage or so close to the actress.

1) Yvette Guilbert, lithograph.
2) Yvette Guilbert, illustration by Lautrec for the album published by Marty with 100 drawings and text by Gustave Geffroy.
3) Yvette Guilbert, 1894 - Plan for a poster on rough paper 186 x 93 cm - Albi, Musée Toulouse-Lautrec.

In 1894, influenced by the opinion of some friends, Yvette Guilbert turned down a poster designed for her by Lautrec (who also dedicated to her five paintings, four watercolours, 24 drawings, 32 lithographs and the silhouette of the Divan Japonais). If one compares the drawings done by Lautrec to those of Yvette made by other artists such as Steinlen, Bac and Ibels, it is obvious that only Lautrec has captured the real spirit and character of the actress.

THE SALON AT
THE RUE DES MOULINS

1894 - Oil on canvas, 110 x 130 cm -
Albi, Musée Toulouse-Lautrec

Between 1894 and 1896, at the same time as his researches into the music halls, Lautrec would install himself at times at the brothel in the Rue des Moulins. He looked at the world of prostitution without prejudice or sentimentality, genuinely concerned to find out the human truths of the women who peopled it. There is neither criticism nor pity in his drawings and paintings: there is only human and artistic empathy, born of the intimacy which comes from sharing daily life and which ignores gratification as much as disdain. (Lautrec quite openly gave the address of the brothel to his closest friends, without any embarrassment). The girls of the house posed for him in their daily attitudes - at rest, at their toilette, asleep, eating - all with absolute naturalness, offering the painter subjects for numerous masterpieces: Lautrec painted about 30 pictures of the life of the brothel, as well as making a beautiful series of lithographs entitled *Elles*, which he

kept hidden for a long time from the public who were not disposed to accept his revelation of the humanity of these girls, condemned as they were by bourgeois society. But Lautrec's pencil and paintbrush manage to purify every subject, even the most risky, saving in every human situation that piece of truth which makes it genuine. He even decorated the brothel of the Rue d'Amboise and created sixteen ornate panels - each one a portrait of a woman, in a medallion surrounded by a floral motif in the rococo style. The lithographic series of *Elles* was eventually well received by the critics.

The diagram shows the scheme of the composition, with the 'diagonal' of the central figure. This determines the spaces to the right and left for the other characters in the scene, the central column and the exact positioning of the figures.

The shades of colour shown are the blood red of the cushions, the purple of the divan, the azure of the slip worn by the central figure, the pale violet of the Madame's dress (as they appear in the picture).

Jean-Louis Renaud wrote in Le Telegramme de Toulouse: "He has painted vice, not because he finds it attractive, since he has avoided obscene details, nor with intent to moralise. He does not attempt to accentuate the ugliness; he has painted it in all its cruel necessity, without smugness, without irony, without inscription: banal, human and sad!"

This is one of the most important of Lautrec's paintings inspired by the life of the prostitutes. In the salon, where it seems we can smell the acid perfume of the thick enclosing air, the large purple divan dominates the scene and upon it recline the girls as they await their clients. The foreshortening, as always, is very modern, with the figure on the right cut off by the frame, the figure in the middle caught in a natural pose, the other girls obviously waiting, while rigidly distinct from them all is the figure of the 'madame' with her sharply characterised expression.

The painting is a 'snap shot' taken from a long series of paintings which he painted throughout his life in a combination of pastels. The red and purple tones of the divan and floor dominate here against which stand out the blue and violet of the girl's clothes in the foreground and the dress of the 'madame'. Once again Lautrec wanted only to record, describe and witness his times, without criticism or irony but with understanding and genuine personal involvement.

Study of heads of girls of the house published with other lithographs in the collection Elles. *Art Moderne of April 26 1896 wrote: "Monsieur Toulouse-Lautrec exhibits at the Plume 11 colour lithographs printed by M.G. Pellet and collected in an album entitled* Elles.

These new works, of which a study was recently seen in Brussels at the 'Free Aesthetics' (exhibition), reproduce with perfect accuracy and charming style episodes from the life of prostitutes. They rank among the best works of the artist and achieve notable success".

MARCELLE LENDER DANCING THE BOLERO IN 'CHILPERIC'

1895 - Oil on canvas, 145 x 150 cm
New York, J.H. Whitney Collection

The scene is from the operetta 'Chilperic', shown at the Théâtre de Variétés in February 1895. Lautrec was so fascinated by the beauty and accomplishment of the actress Marcelle Lender that he returned to see it about 20 times, filling his notebook with sketches from which he eventually produced this canvas - fireworks of rhythm and colours. In the volume *Lautrec par Lautrec* by Huisman and Dortu, Marcelle Lender herself recalls how the painting came about.

"Contrary to custom, Lautrec did not compliment me on my talent, nor on my part in the 'Chilperic' that he had just seen. He never stopped watching me, with embarrassing intensity. He ate a little ham and a whole jar of gherkins. He poured himself glasses of burgundy, which he drank in one go. When he started to talk to me again he was charming, but sometimes dismissive. But he ended up by amusing us all and came back for supper three times in a row. One day, after the second act in which I dance the fandango, a bunch of white roses was brought to me with a note from the artist. He asked for a rendezvous; I replied that he should come to lunch with me two days later. Lautrec livens up a meal in an extraordinary way: his vivacity is inexhaustible. He took his leave of me before I could work out the reason he had wanted to see me. He returned to the Variétés several times and came to see me in my dressing room. Two months later his picture of the dance in 'Chilperic' was finished".

In the same year in which he painted the great canvas of the dance in 'Chilperic', Lautrec made other portraits of Lender, amongst which are these two lithographs showing the dancer in profile as she takes a bow (left) and from the front (below).

CHA-U-KAO, THE FEMALE CLOWN

1895 - Oil on canvas, 75 x 55 cm - Winterthur, Oscar Reinhart Collection

This painting shows the female clown Cha-U-Kao on the arm of the dancer Gabrielle (this subject was repeated by Toulouse-Lautrec in a colour lithograph of March 1897, 20 copies of which were printed by Pellet and published in Figaro Illustré in 1901); in the background, in profile, is the writer Tristan Bernard. If the painter has left us images of Yvette Guilbert that show a theatrical intelligence, in the clown Cha-U-Kao Lautrec reveals a sorrowful nature, a resigned and pathetic melancholy. Dancer, acrobat, clown and woman of easy virtue, Cha-U-Kao, who claimed to be Japanese, performed at the Nouveau-Cirque and at the Moulin Rouge. Her oriental-sounding stage name in fact stands for Uproar-Chaos (Chahut-Chaos). The picture plays on the contrast between the vivid colour in the outlandish get-up of the clown (with cheeky yellow blouse and green-blue trousers distinctively contrasted) and the shadow of her eyes brimming with unspoken tenderness and sadness

The diagram shows the diagonal lines that 'guide' the placing and posture of the central figures, according to a perfect, instinctive equilibrium.

hidden behind the make-up and sequins of the actresses and dancers. It is a melancholy that demonstrates the painter's own understanding and empathy towards the figures who inhabit the world which he chose as his home and which he painted with a perceptiveness and intuition no previous artist had ever shown.

The details show the principal characters of the painting: the dancer Gabrielle, Cha-U-Kao, and Tristan Bernard, lawyer and writer. He met Lautrec during the staging of the Revue Blanche and he introduced him to the sporting world, enabling him to meet the most famous cyclists of the time. As in all his work, Toulouse-Lautrec pays attention to the physiological and psychological aspects of each character, as well as their profound individuality

MADEMOISELLE EGLANTINE'S TROUPE

1896 - Board, 73 x 92 cm - Turin, Private Collection

Only an extraordinary capacity for instant observation and his personal technique of drawing with chalk and coloured pencils made it possible for Toulouse-Lautrec to capture in his sketch the frenzied movements of the can-can. Lautrec loved drawing on card, using the neutral tone of the background to integrate the rapid sketches: thus the blue lines of the broad shapes of the blouses and hats, and the rounded whites of the faces and white of the petticoats stand out against the grey-ochre of the card. This simple sketch (a study for the poster shown above right) tells us, as though it were far more than a simple painting of Lautrec's world, much about his style of drawing and his amazing technique. In those rapid chalk strokes and pencil lines we find not only movement - the swirling of skirts, the music of the famous dance - we discover also the personality of each dancer,

(from left: Jane Avril, Cleopatre, Eglantine, Gazelle). The features and expression of the faces are captured precisely despite his swiftness of execution. There is above all, the originality of the painter's point of observation looking across and up at the stage and the dancers performing on it.

Above: La Troupe De Mademoiselle Eglantine, colour poster for an English tour - 1896 61.5 x 80 cm.

Dance At The Moulin Rouge, 1890 - Oil on canvas, 115 x 150 cm - Philadelphia, Collection of Henry P. McIlhenny. As in the pictures inspired by the world of the Moulin Rouge, Lautrec portrayed real people, picking out their characteristics and features. At the centre of the scene Valentin le Désossé and La Goulue dance together; beside La Goulue are the painters and photographers Varney, Maxime Guilbert, Sescan and Gauzi; on the right with the beard is the painter's father; facing is Jane Avril, wrapped in a dark cape.

AT THE BAR

1898 - Oil on board, 82 x 60 cm - Zurich, Kunsthaus

On this large board, the colour of which forms the base colour for the painting, Toulouse-Lautrec depicts two anonymous people in a cafe. With a brush that both draws and paints, using large rapid strokes, the painter succeeds in capturing the impression that struck him. We can almost see him as he passes in front of the bar, glancing casually round. He looks more closely, then retraces his steps and picks up one of the sketch boards that he always carries with him. In a few minutes he captures the image of the fat man with a red moustache beside the cashier. Almost half of the board is taken up by the bar on which a bottle and glass rest (a few strokes of white and blue); on the right is the till. The rest of the painting is filled by the mass of the man in the brown coat and the figure of the woman, dressed in blue. Beside the round face of the man, with the red hair and whiskers, is the sharp outline of the cashier's profile, emerging from her white frilly collar.

With his extraordinary capacity for synthesis Lautrec does not shy away from fully depicting the space of the scene, painting the reflections of the characters' heads in the mirror behind them. Several things strike one about the painting, apart from its immediacy and freshness. The actual point of view of the painter, just a little higher than the bar; the shading of the ground that becomes brown in the man's coat, then mixes with the green of the walls behind the two people; the transparency of the bottle and glass; the blue of the cashier's dress and the white of her collar; the colouring of the faces, in particular the pallor of the woman's face in profile.

The point of view chosen by the painter is his actual one. Lautrec gives half the board's space to representing the bar, and only the upper half to the two figures.
The painter drew every fact that interested him, searching for expression, character, mystery and the meaning of their inner life . "Only the human form exists", he used to say to his friends, "landscape should be nothing but an accessory, the landscape painter is only a primitive. Landscape should serve only to give a greater understanding of the character of the figure".

At Hannetton's or At The Brasserie 1898, Lithograph

Right: Reine De Joie, 1892 - poster for the book of the same name by Victor Joze.

WOMAN AT HER TOILETTE: MADAME POUPOULE

1899-1900 - Oil on panel, 60.8 x 49.6cm - Albi, Musée Toulouse-Lautrec.

This painting shows Lautrec's mature style in which he demonstrates a rare feeling for his materials and the expressive potential of colour. Lautrec painted the girl at the brothel many times, leaving, beside this image, another as if in 'reverse shot'- that is, from behind while she looks at herself in the mirror, her long loose hair falling over her shoulders. Perhaps, from among the many girls of the house, the painter was attracted by her mass of long reddish-brown hair hiding her childish face. In this painting the colour of her red hair stands out against the changing green of the housecoat which is reflected in the small crystal bottles on her dressing table.

Here, more than in other works, the surface of the painting acquires a significance while the base also stands out. Lautrec places colour upon the neutral base of the board, leaving the background to show through where he intends to suggest transparency and reflection, as, for example on the girl's right arm or on the wall.

As always, there are few colours: all the harmony of the picture is based

The English Barmaid At The Star At Le Havre, 1899 - Oil on panel, 41 x 33 cm - Albi, Musée Toulouse-Lautrec. This is one of Lautrec's last works. The painter met this English girl, who inspired him to paint with extraordinary freshness and expressivity, in the 'Star', a cafe at Le Havre. Many aspects are striking about this incisive portrait of Miss Dolly - the aggressive colours, the speed of the brushstrokes, the contrast of her blond hair against the blues of her dress and the background, the evocative geometry of the background built up by the weaving and superimposing of planes of colour.

on the relationship between the warm tones of the cylindrical box in the foreground, of the back of the mirror, of the wall, above all of Madame Poupoule's hair, the neutral colour of her dress and the cold off-white rather dirty tones of the table top.

HOW DOES LAUTREC SET TO WORK?
1) With red chalk Lautrec sketches the figure of the girl, busy doing her nails, making use of the background colour.
2) He then adds rapid strokes of blue and green mixed with white, letting through the colour of the panel to paint the clothes with an effect of transparency.
3) Beside the cold tones of the table and the clothes, he adds touches and brushstrokes of warm shades for the wall, the face and the hair. On the small bottles in the background, to the left, a few brushstrokes of blue render the reflection of the clothing.

A DOWN-TO-EARTH ARTIST

Toulouse-Lautrec's Paris has become a city of legend. The bitter-sweet chanteuses, the can-can dancers, the parade of the fashionably dressed with the ever-present hint of erotic encounters unite to create an unforgettable image of the carefree city. That we know Lautrec was a part of this life adds to the appeal of his works, for they seem to be fresh, spontaneous moments from his life, vivid glimpses of groups at nearby tables or in a bar, or of dancers strolling past him on their way to the dance floor. We participate in his pleasures as he effortlessly introduces us to the world he inhabited. Seldom has there appeared to be such a simple transition between life and art.

Certainly Lautrec is one of the most down-to-earth of artists, for there is nothing escapist, sentimental or nostalgic in anything he did. His source was always the present world immediately around him. Yet, like all great art which seems simple, great sophistication and considerable artifice underlay it. Lautrec learnt many of his techniques from Degas. It was Degas who discovered from early photography that, in glimpses of real life - as opposed to carefully arranged paintings - parts of figures could be cut off, fragments of figures appear at the sides or bodies appear cropped at top and bottom. Further, the camera showed that, when not viewed full-frontally as in most paintings, the various perspectives of the space around us often assume disconcerting or surprising angles.

A DRAMATIC PAINTER

Lautrec, like Degas, used this technique most dramatically in theatrical scenes where different

TOULOUSE- LAUTREC AND HIS TIMES

	HIS LIFE AND WORK	HISTORY	ARTS AND CULTURE
1864	Born 24 November at Albi	Founding of the Red Cross at Geneva Act against sending child chimney sweeps up chimneys Marx and Engels found the First International	Dostoyevsky: *Notes From Underground* Baudelaire finishes *My Heart Laid Bare* Rodin's *Man With A Broken Nose* rejected by the Salon
1878	He has his first fall, and a second a year later. Because of a bone illness, his legs will not grow after these falls	At the Congress of Berlin, Prime Minister Disraeli checks Russian expansion in the Balkans J Swann invents the electric light bulb	Degas: *Dancers Taking A Curtain Call* Monet: *Saint-Lazare Gare*
1882	After a year's study in the studio of Princeteau, a great horse painter, he returns to Bonnat, an academic painter, but is influenced by Impressionism	Death of Garibaldi Death of Charles Darwin Phoenix Park murders in Dublin worsen Anglo-Irish relations	Birth of James Joyce Birth of Virginia Woolf Manet: *The Bar At The Folies Bergère*
1884	He enters the studio of Cormon. He becomes friends with Emile Bernard, Anquetin and Grenier. He haunts the bars, dancehalls, theatres and brothels of Montmartre	Petrol motor invented Third Reform Act of Parliament gives vote to all rural households General Gordon besieged in Khartoum by the Mahdi; Gordon killed the following year	Foundation of the Salon des Indépendants, where Seurat exhibits *La Baignade* Huysmans: *Against Nature*
1886	He leaves the family home and rents a studio in Rue Tourlaque (which he will keep until 1897). He gets to know Aristide Bruant; friendship with Van Gogh whom he meets at Cormon's	Third Ministry of William Gladstone introduces Home Rule Bill for Ireland - rejected in the House of Lords Gold discovered on the Rand in South Africa attracts influx of immigrants, fuelling the Boers' resentment	Death of Franz Liszt Pierre Lotti: *The Island Fishers*
1888	*Bareback rider at Fernando's,* his first big work. He exhibits at the Salon of XX at Brussels	Cecil Rhodes acquires the future Rhodesia (now Zimbabwe) Local Government Act sets up County Councils in England and Wales	Birth of T. S. Eliot Maupassant: *Pierre Et Jean*
1889	*The Laundress* with Carmen Gaudin as model. *At The Moulin De La Galette* his second big work, influenced by Japanese art. He exhibits at the Salon des Indépendants	World Fair in Paris Dockers win their first all-out strike	Tolstoy: *The Kreutzer Sonata* Richard Strauss: *Don Juan* Edvard Munch starts *The Frieze Of Life*

positions around the theatre can give dramatic angles onto the stage, orchestra or auditorium. Lautrec realised this was particularly effective in posters, which by their nature call for bold effects. Perhaps the best example of this comes in his *Divan Japonais* poster (see page 12), where we seem to be part of the audience, sitting with a couple in their box, with the steep angle of the stage and of the orchestra pit before us, out of which peer the surreal heads of the double basses. In the top left corner is the headless fragment of a performer in the spotlight. But she has no need of a head, for her long black gloves tell us she is the singer Yvette Guilbert.

Apart from Degas, Impressionism influenced Lautrec only in his student years and then primarily through the art of Edouard Manet. Significantly for Lautrec's art, Manet was, after Degas, the Impressionist painter most concerned with painting the human form. Many of his paintings, such as *Dejeuner Sur L'Herbe*, had caused a scandal when first exhibited for their frank, unsentimental depiction of human sexuality.

Lautrec indeed, apart from a few very early pictures from his pre-Paris days, showed no interest in landscape painting at all, regarding it as an inferior art form, "fit only for primitives". Pictures without people lacked interest for Lautrec; more than this, he was drawn always to the artificial, the man-made, rather than to the natural: to the artificially lit night club with all its grotesque possibilities, rather than the simple life in a country cottage. The exception was his fascination with horses - an inheritance perhaps from his sporting ancestors.

Nor could he share the

1890	*Dance At The Moulin Rouge*, where La Goulue triumphs	Parnell Scandal: Charles Parnell, leader of the Irish nationalists, falls from power after being named in a divorce case	Oscar Wilde: *The Picture Of Dorian Grey* Debussy sets *Five Poems Of Baudelaire* to music
1891	First poster: *The Dance At The Moulin Rouge*. He exhibits at the Salon des XX	Creation of the Pan-German union signifies increasing German nationalism	Herman Melville: *Billy Budd* Paul Gauguin paints *On The Beach*
1892	*At The Moulin Rouge*, new large work First lithograph showing *La Goulue On The Arms Of Her Sister*	Gladstone becomes PM for the fourth and last time; tries to introduce Home Rule for Ireland bill, again defeated in House of Lords Panama Canal financial scandal in France	Norman Shaw builds Chesters, Northumberland Rudyard Kipling: *Barrack Room Ballads* Oscar Wilde: *Lady Windermere's Fan* Paul Cézanne: *The Card Players*
1895	He finishes *The Salon At The Rue Des Moulins*, a resumé and study of his experiences of brothels. He paints *Marcel Lender Dancing The Bolero Of 'Chilperic', Two Friends Of The Clown Cha-U-Kao* He takes part in the first Art Nouveau Salon	Rontgen discovers X rays Trial and imprisonment of Oscar Wilde	Rudyard Kipling: *The Jungle Book* (part 2) Oscar Wilde: *The Importance Of Being Earnest* Sigmund Freud: *Studies in Hysteria* Birth of Robert Graves
1896	Travels to Holland, Belgium	Dreyfus affair starts in France First modern Olympic Games in Athens	Puccini: *La Bohème*
1898	He does eight lithographs of Yvette Guilbert for a London album He is at the height of his powers	Battle of Omdurman: Kitchener defeats the Mahdi Marie Curie discovers radium	Oscar Wilde; *The Ballad of Reading Gaol* H.G. Wells: *War of the Worlds* Birth of George Gershwin
1899	In the month of February he is interned at Folie-Saint-James de Neuilly to undergo a 'drying out' cure. Freed in May, he resumes his life as before	The rehabilitation of Dreyfus The Boxer rising in China	W.B . Yeats: *The Wind In The Reeds* Maurice Ravel: *Pavane For A Dead Infanta* Edwin Lutyens builds Deanery Gardens
1900	He paints *The Modiste* and *Messalina Seated*	New World Fair at Paris Founding of the Independent Labour Party	Triumph of Art Nouveau at Paris World Fair
1901	He paints his last work *An Examination At The Faculty Of Medicine*. Paralysed, he dies 9 September at Malromé	President MacKinley assassinated in USA; Theodore Roosevelt succeeds him	Thomas Mann: *Buddenbroks* Anton Chekov: *The Three Sisters* Rudyard Kipling: *Kim*

Impressionists' almost scientific investigation of natural light and their reliance on distinctive broken brushwork to further it. To Lautrec's generation of painters, the Post-Impressionists, a group of widely differing individuals, the Impressionists seemed to have reached a dead-end. Each of the succeeding generation, in spirited reaction against Impressionism, set out to find their own way forward: Gauguin renounced "the abominable error of naturalism"; Cézanne wished to create something "solid and endurable" and succeeded with the triumphant solidity of his mature landscapes; Van Gogh strove to "express man's terrible passions" through overboiling intensities of line and colour; Seurat continued the Impressionists' cool analysis of colour.

Lautrec used Seurat's style in *Jane Avril Leaving The Moulin Rouge* (see page 6) but chiefly for decorative effect, with a gold background scintillating in a manner Seurat never attempted. Like most of his contemporaries, he turned towards stronger design and graphic qualities. As a painter, he favoured the use of thin paint applied to board, a technique which naturally favoured a smoother surface finish. He also tended to compose by combining a number of flat shapes. So an important painting like *At The Moulin Rouge* (see pages 10-11) is made up of the forms of the coats and hats, even of whole figures in the background, which fit together in a pattern almost independent of the perspective of the picture.

GAUGUIN THE PIONEER

This technique had been pioneered by Paul Gauguin about the time Lautrec was attending Cormon's classes. It was continued in the 1890s by a group of Gauguin's followers called the Nabis, many of whom were Lautrec's friends. All these artists had looked back to a source Degas had also plundered - Japanese art. Lautrec collected the Japanese prints enormously popular among artists at the time; his enthusiasm was such that his mother even offered to pay for his passage to Japan. In homage Lautrec turned his initials into a little oriental hieroglyph, which looked like the signature stamps of Japanese printmakers, and he too used it to sign his graphic works.

It was of course the graphic design element of Japanese prints that attracted Lautrec. He loved the way large bright-coloured parts of the print were flattened out by the absence of shading and drawn together by flowing elegant outlines. The great Japanese printmakers were masters of simplification, able to reduce the essence of a figure to a few lines. This was just the sort of accuracy Lautrec sought as the epitome of his witty, sophisticated style.

Japanese influence was rife in Paris at the time, spilling over from the fine arts into fabrics, furniture and ceramics. Siegfried Bing, the important Parisian dealer in oriental art, had set up a gallery to promote the renaissance of decorative art which was influenced partly by the Japanese example. He called it Art Nouveau and Lautrec can also be seen in some ways as an Art Nouveau artist, particularly in his commercial work such as posters, advertisements, programmes or illustrations. The decorative curving, swirling line which he loved to use, brought out in women's hair and dress, was indeed an Art Nouveau line ubiquitous in Paris at the time, from newly-built Metro stations down to small pieces of jewelry.

Lautrec was so open to the world around him that it would be odd if there were no traces of Art Nouveau in his work. But, more than this, in his posters seen all over the city, he was also one of the principal creators of the graphic style. Further, unlike many of his predecessors, he was not confined to painting but was also a master printer. It was typical of the age that he felt the need to extend his range beyond the fine arts into commercial work. This reveals not only his utter lack of artistic snobbery but also the enhanced status of the minor arts due to the Art Nouveau Revolution.

This sense of freedom to work in whatever way he wanted is part of Lautrec's whole attitude to his life and art. In Paris he felt as much at ease at a smart social gathering of the nobility as he did in bars or brothels and he painted and drew whatever he saw with an impartial lack of discrimination. When he was enjoying himself, the results were some of the most exhilarating pictures ever painted, but he viewed the darker side of life with the same unblinking gaze. The loneliness and melancholy that he often detected in his performers - especially in the bored whores of the Rue des Moulins brothel or the exhausted danseuses of the Moulin Rouge - is a poetic counterpoint to the exuberance of so much of his work. Lautrec's sensitivity also makes him a modern artist. It was this which was picked up, soon after his death, by the young Picasso's wistful pierrots and clowns.